Reading fo

Reading Comprehension Book
Reading Level 2.0–3.5

Introduction

Welcome to the Edupress Reading for Detail Reading Comprehension Book. This resource is an effective tool for instruction, practice, and evaluation of student understanding. It includes ideas on how to introduce reading for detail to students, as well as activities to help teach and practice the concept.

The reproducible activities in this book are tailored to individual, small-group, and whole-class work. They include leveled reading passages, graphic organizers, worksheets, and detailed instruction pages. These activities provide opportunities to use text, illustrations, graphics, and combinations of these elements to practice identifying details in text.

The material in this book is written for readers at the 2.0–3.5 reading level. However, the activities can easily be adapted to your students' ability levels and your time frame. After introducing an activity to students, model it by working through one or two examples aloud. You may wish to also read text passages aloud to students, or they can be read silently or aloud by students. For students who need personalized help, individual and small-group activities have been included. These activities can be done alone or with a classroom aide for explicit instruction.

We know you will be pleased with the progress your students make in reading for details after using this book.

ISBN 13: 978-1-56472-158-7

www.edupressinc.com

Table of Contents

Directions: Reading for Details

Whole Class 

Introduce the idea of reading for details. Read a short picture book, such as *Where the Wild Things Are*. Ask students for the boy's name. Then, ask where his mother sent him when he misbehaved. Finally, ask what meal he ate at the end of the story.

Next, write the titles "Shawn's Surprise" and "A New Boy in Class" on the board. Ask a volunteer to read both aloud. Explain that these are the titles of two different stories. Encourage the students to predict what they think each story might be about. Record the students' ideas on a chart, on the board, or on an overhead transparency. List vocabulary words that come up in the discussion.

Reproduce "Shawn's Surprise" on page 4 and "A New Boy in Class" on page 6 for each student and give the class time to read. Ask how the actual stories were different from their original predictions. Record student responses. Add vocabulary not included in the original list.

Small Group 

Reproduce "Shawn's Surprise" for each student in half the class and "A New Boy in Class" for the other half. Use one color of paper for each story so the two tales will be easy to differentiate from a distance.

Instruct students to read the stories silently. Encourage each reader to review the material carefully and write down important details. Explain that these notes are very important. Tell them that they will be retelling the stories to other students. Their listeners will be expected to answer questions about details.

When students are ready, collect the colored pages. Match each reader of "Shawn's Surprise" with a classmate who has read and prepared notes for "A New Boy in Class."

First, readers of "Shawn's Surprise" should tell the story based on their notes. When the storytellers finish, distribute the comprehension question sheets on page 5 to each of their listeners.

After answering the questions, the listeners become storytellers. They use their notes to tell "A New Boy in Class." Distribute the comprehension questions on page 7 to their partners.

Allow each partner to read the other story and revise the comprehension answers, if necessary.

Answer Key

"Shawn's Surprise" Questions (Page 5)

1. He wanted to know what his surprise was.
2. The Corner Café
3. Shawn's friend
4. dinosaurs
5. He is the best artist in class.
6. Little League
7. Monday
8. gumballs
9. Brenda Holiday
10. beagle puppies
11. milk and sliced apples
12. His father is coming home next week.

"A New Boy in Class" Questions (Page 7)

1. A new student was standing at the door.
2. Tina
3. Blake Carlson
4. show Blake around the school
5. the library
6. All students had their own computers.
7. Alaska
8. 10 students
9. The boys were making noise in the hallway.
10. He tricked Sam into explaining basketball to him.
11. His brother won a basketball scholarship.
12. Answers may vary.

Shawn's Surprise

Shawn shifted his weight from one foot to the other. The "walk" signal finally came on. He hurried across the street.

Then, he heard a familiar voice shout, "Wait for me!"

Shawn stopped and turned around. His friend Addison caught up with him.

"What's the rush?" Addison asked, gasping for breath.

"My mom called. There's a surprise for me at home," Shawn said.

"What is it?" Addison asked.

"If I knew, it wouldn't be a surprise," Shawn said.

The friends walked by The Corner Café. The window was filled with pictures of dinosaurs. Addison pointed to them. "Didn't you enter that coloring contest? You're the best artist in our class. Maybe you won," she said.

"No, the contest doesn't end until next week," Shawn said.

"Oh," Addison said.

The friends walked on down the street. They passed the playing field at Greenland Park. "Didn't you try out for the Little League team? Maybe you made it," Addison said.

"No, the tryouts were just last weekend. Coach Wilson won't call until next Monday," Shawn said.

"Oh," Addison said.

The kids came to Tucker's Toyshop. They stopped to look in the window. There was a big jar filled with gumballs.

"Maybe you guessed the right number," Addison said.

Shawn pointed to a little sign beside the jar. It said "593 gumballs. Brenda Holiday wins a $50 gift certificate for her guess of 590 gumballs."

"Guess not," Addison said.

Next, the friends came to the pet store. Two beagle puppies were playing in the window. Addison paused to watch them, but Shawn just kept walking. Addison had to run to catch up.

"You're really in a hurry," Addison said.

"Mom's really excited. I can tell. This is an important surprise," Shawn said.

"It isn't the coloring contest. It isn't Little League team, and it isn't the gumball jar. What could it be?" Addison wondered.

"I don't know," Shawn said.

"Maybe it's a puppy," Addison said.

"No, my sister is allergic to dogs," Shawn said.

"I give up," Addison said.

"Here's my house. Why don't you come in and find out?" Shawn asked.

"Hello, kids," said Shawn's mother. She brought them some milk and sliced apples. Then, she handed Shawn an envelope.

Shawn's heart beat faster. It was addressed to him. It was from his father. He ripped it open and read the letter.

"What is it?" Addison demanded.

"Dad's coming home next week. That's the best surprise ever!" he said.

"Shawn's Surprise" Questions

Name: ______________________

1. Why was Shawn hurrying? ______________________
2. What was the first place the friends walked past? ______________________
3. Who is Addison? ______________________
4. Shawn entered a picture in a coloring contest. What kind of animals were in the picture? ______________________
5. Addison thought Shawn won the coloring contest. Why? ______________________
6. Shawn tried out for a team. What kind of team was it? ______________________
7. When was Coach Wilson going to call? ______________________
8. What was in the jar at the toy shop? ______________________
9. Who won the gumball guessing contest? ______________________
10. What did the kids see at the pet shop? ______________________
11. What did Shawn's mother give the kids to eat? ______________________
12. What was Shawn's surprise? ______________________

A New Boy in Class

Sam poked Mike in the arm. His friend looked up from reading his book.

"What?" Mike whispered.

Sam pointed toward the doorway. A tall boy was standing there. He was holding a piece of yellow paper. Those slips came from the office. They were for new students.

"He is going to be in our class. I wonder if he likes basketball. Our team needs a good forward," Mike said.

Tina, the girl in front of Mike, turned around and glared at him.

Mrs. Melvin stood up. Mike thought he was in trouble, but he wasn't.

The teacher walked straight over to the door. She took the yellow slip from the boy. "This is Blake Carlson. He will be joining our class," she said.

Sam raised his hand. "May I show him where everything is?" he asked.

"What a good idea!" Mrs. Melvin said.

Sam closed his book and hurried up to meet the new boy.

"I'm Sam Martin. I'm sure you'll like it here. Come on, I'll show you around," he said.

The two boys walked down the quiet hallway. "This is the library," Sam said.

"Do you have computers?" Blake asked.

"Sure, they're in the lab next door," Sam said.

"We had our own computers at my other school. We had access to the Internet, too," Blake said.

"Really?" Sam asked.

Blake nodded. Sam led the new boy out into the lunch area.

"Where was your school?" Sam asked.

"In a little town in Alaska. There were 10 students. I was the only one in the third grade. My brother was in high school. We were all in the same class," Blake said.

"A small school, huh? I guess that means you didn't have a basketball team," Sam said. He tried not to sound disappointed.

"Basketball? What's that?" Blake asked.

"It's a game..." Sam began.

Blake started to laugh. One of the first-grade teachers came over to her classroom window, glared at the boys, and then slammed the window shut. Blake put his hand over his mouth.

Blake shrugged. "Sorry, I couldn't help it," he whispered.

"What was so funny?" Sam whispered.

"You were trying to tell me about basketball. Winters in Alaska were so cold and dark that we couldn't go outside for months. We played basketball in the town gym. We moved here because my brother was offered a college basketball scholarship."

Sam put his hand on Blake's shoulder. "I knew it! You're going to win for us," he said.

"I don't know about that. Winning takes a whole team," Blake said.

"We have a great team, and you'll meet them at recess," Sam said.

"You were right. I'm going to like it here," Blake said.

Whispering, the two new friends hurried back to class.

"A New Boy in Class" Questions

Name: ______________________

1. Why did Sam poke Mike in the arm? ______________________
2. Who glared at Mike? ______________________
3. What was the new boy's name? ______________________
4. What did Sam offer to do? ______________________
5. Where did Sam take Blake first? ______________________
6. Every student had something special at Blake's old school. What was it? ______________________
7. Where was Blake's old school? ______________________
8. How big was Blake's old school? ______________________
9. Why did the teacher close her window? ______________________
10. Why did Blake laugh? ______________________
11. Why did Blake's family move? ______________________
12. Do you think Blake was a good player? Give reasons for your answer. ______________________

Directions: Scientific Details

Individual ●

Reproduce "Turtles" on page 9 or "The Water Cycle" on page 10, along with the Thinking First Graphic Organizer on page 11, for each student. Have students study the article's title and then use the title and prior knowledge to fill in the first and second boxes of the organizer. Next, encourage them to read the text. They should use any information they discover to fill in the third box. In the last box, they should add sources for additional information about turtles or the water cycle. For example, they might include books, an encyclopedia, or websites.

Small Group ●●

Divide students into groups of three or four. Reproduce "Turtles" or "The Water Cycle" and the graphic organizer for each group. Encourage group members to discuss the title of the story, and then have them fill in the first two boxes of the graphic organizer. Next, students should take turns reading the article aloud. When they have finished reading, have them work together to fill in the remaining boxes in the organizer. Encourage each group to use the graphic organizer to report what they have learned to the class.

Whole Class 

Reproduce "Turtles" or "The Water Cycle" and the graphic organizer on transparencies. Display the graphic organizer and hold a class brainstorming session. For example, ask students what they know about turtles and what they want to know. Then, read the article as a class. Ask students what they have learned. Then, challenge them to think of other questions that were not covered in the article. Ask where they could find answers to these questions. Finish filling in the graphic organizer.

As an extension, encourage students to use the information they have recorded to create a brochure or newsletter.

Turtles

Turtles are reptiles. Lizards and snakes belong to the same group, or class, of animals. All reptiles have some common traits: They lay eggs, and they have scales on their bodies. They also have lungs to breathe air, and they are ectothermic. That means their body temperature is the same as the air around them.

Turtles are the only reptiles with shells. Scientists call them chelonians. That name comes from a Greek word for "tortoise." There are about 250 species, or kinds, of turtles. Some are as long as a classroom table. Others would fit into the palm of your hand.

Turtles can be found almost everywhere in the world, except Antarctica. They live in deserts, seas, rain forests, lakes, and streams. They even live in backyard ponds.

Some kinds of turtles spend their whole lives on the land. They are called tortoises. These land turtles can live for many years. Harriet, a Galapagos tortoise, lived in the Australia Zoo. She was 176 years old when she died! Adwaita, a tortoise in India, might have been even older.

Galapagos tortoises are the largest land turtles. Some weigh more than 900 pounds! That is about the same as a large black bear.

Tortoises move slowly. They travel only about one mile every two hours, but they don't have to be fast. They don't run away from danger. Instead, they hide inside their shells. They don't have to chase their food because they eat grass, cacti, or leaves.

Tortoises can't swim. If a land turtle falls into a pond, it will sink. Most other turtles do not have that problem. They have webbed feet and are great swimmers. The leatherback turtle can swim more than 20 miles per hour. It can also dive to depths of 3,000 feet.

Leatherbacks spend most of their lives in the ocean. Mother leatherbacks crawl up on land only to lay their eggs. Leatherback shells are not as hard as tortoise shells. Staying near their nests would not be safe. Mother turtles cover and hide their eggs with sand. Then, they hurry back to the water.

Some turtles, called terrapins, are at home in the water, but they also like to sit on sunny rocks. Terrapins live near rivers, marshes, or ponds.

Many species of turtles are endangered. People are their greatest enemies. The places where turtles live are no longer safe. This is because too many roads and houses are being built. Even trash in the water can kill turtles. Scientists are looking for ways to protect these amazing animals.

The Water Cycle

From space, Earth looks like a blue ball. Our planet's oceans, rivers, and lakes make it special. Earth is the only planet in our solar system with so much liquid water.

We take water for granted, but it is very important. In fact, water makes life possible. About two-thirds of the human body is water. People can live for weeks without food but only a few days without water.

Water moves and changes form all the time. These changes are called the water cycle. A cycle has no beginning or end. The following example can help you understand how the water cycle works.

A mountain rainstorm ends. Storm water roars over rocks in the creek. It races down to a river in the valley. That river joins other rivers. Some of the water from the storm flows into the ocean.

Not all of the storm water runs off. Some of it collects in puddles under the trees. Dragonflies, gnats, and bees come to drink. When the sun comes out, these pools dry up.

Some of the water soaks into the ground. Tree roots take it in. Special cells in the trunks pull water and minerals up to the leaves.

The rest of the water disappears, too. It turns into droplets too small to see. Warm, dry air carries the drops away. This is called evaporation.

Warm air carrying the tiny water drops rises over the treetops. It rises above the mountain peaks. As it rises, it cools. When the air cools, the water drops cling together. They grab onto bits of dust. A mist forms. This is called condensation. It is the beginning of a cloud.

The cloud grows. More water droplets join together. They become too heavy for the air, and they fall back to Earth. This is called precipitation.

In the summer, precipitation is usually rain. But thunderstorms can also drop chunks of ice called hail. Hailstones can be dangerous. They can reach speeds of 100 miles per hour as they fall.

On cold winter days, something different happens inside clouds. Water freezes into beautiful crystals and drifts down as snow.

So while it may seem complicated, the water cycle is actually simple. Water falls as rain, hail, or snow. It evaporates, then condenses to form a cloud. Finally, it returns to Earth as precipitation. The water cycle makes life on Earth possible.

Thinking First Graphic Organizer

Name:

What we know:

What we want to find out:

What we learned:

How we can learn more:

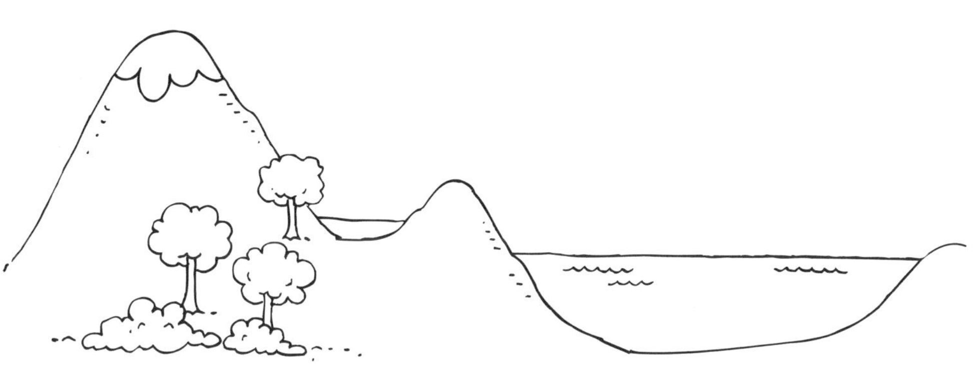

Directions: Finding Sensory Details

Individual ●

This exercise encourages students to look for sensory details in a short story. Reproduce "A Day at the Shore" on page 13 and the Shoreline Senses Graphic Organizer on page 14 for each student. Review the five senses before distributing the selections. Emphasize that the skin is a very large organ. It covers not only fingertips, but also arms, legs, feet, and faces. This means that the sense of touch is experienced in many ways. Remind students that this sense provides information about heat and cold as well as texture. Instruct students to read the story and then write down as many sensory details as they can in the graphic organizer.

When all students have finished, collect and correct the organizers. There should be at least one example of each sense. Careful readers will find more.

Small Group/Whole Class ●●/●●●

Divide the class in half or into small groups. Reproduce "A Day at the Shore" and the graphic organizer for half of the students or small groups. Have them read the story and fill in the graphic organizer. When all students have finished, collect the completed graphic organizers. Distribute them to students who did not read the story.

Challenge the second half of the class to write a story based on the completed graphic organizer. When they finish writing, collect the stories and the organizers. Read "A Day at the Shore" aloud. Then, share some of the student stories.

Offer students an opportunity to discuss the student stories. Invite them to point out ways their stories are the same as "A Day at the Shore." Then, encourage them to give examples of ways each story differs. Call on volunteers to share what they learned from this experience.

A Day at the Shore

"Hurry up," Darrell's mother called. "Mike and his family are waiting for you."

"I can't find my swim trunks," Darrell yelled back.

"They're already in the car. So is your kite. Come on," she said.

Darrell raced down the stairs two at a time. Hot air hit him the minute he opened the front door. Air-conditioning was great—until you went outside! But it would be different at the beach.

His mom was standing on the porch. She was talking to Mike's mom.

Mike was waving from the back window of the van. Darrell ran to join him. The van door slid open with a screech. "That needs a little oil," said Mr. Anderson.

Soon, they were rolling down the highway. Mrs. Anderson popped a CD into the player. A cheerful version of "On Top of Spaghetti" filled the car. Mike sang along, and Darrell joined in. Mr. and Mrs. Anderson sang, too. Two songs later, they pulled into the parking lot.

When he stepped out, Darrell took a deep breath. The cool breeze smelled of salt, seaweed, french fries, burning charcoal, and suntan lotion. Mike sniffed the air and looked around. He pointed toward a refreshment stand at the edge of the parking lot. "Can we buy hot dogs?" he begged.

"No, but you can help me carry the ice chest over to the picnic table," his mom said.

"Oh, okay," he grumbled.

Darrell couldn't complain when Mr. Anderson opened the chest. There were thick turkey sandwiches, crisp vegetables with tangy ranch dip, and sweet sliced oranges for dessert.

After lunch, Darrell and Mike built a sand castle in the damp sand near the water. It had a moat and three towers. Mr. Anderson took lots of pictures with his cell phone. He sent them to Darrell's mom. She sent a message back. She loved them.

They all took a walk down the beach at sunset. The sun drew a long, bright line across the water. It pointed right toward them. When the sun sank below the horizon, the sky turned orange and red. The water turned red, too.

The van felt cozy and warm when Darrell and Mike climbed into the backseat. They headed home under a starry sky. It had been a perfect day.

Shoreline Senses Graphic Organizer

Name:_______________

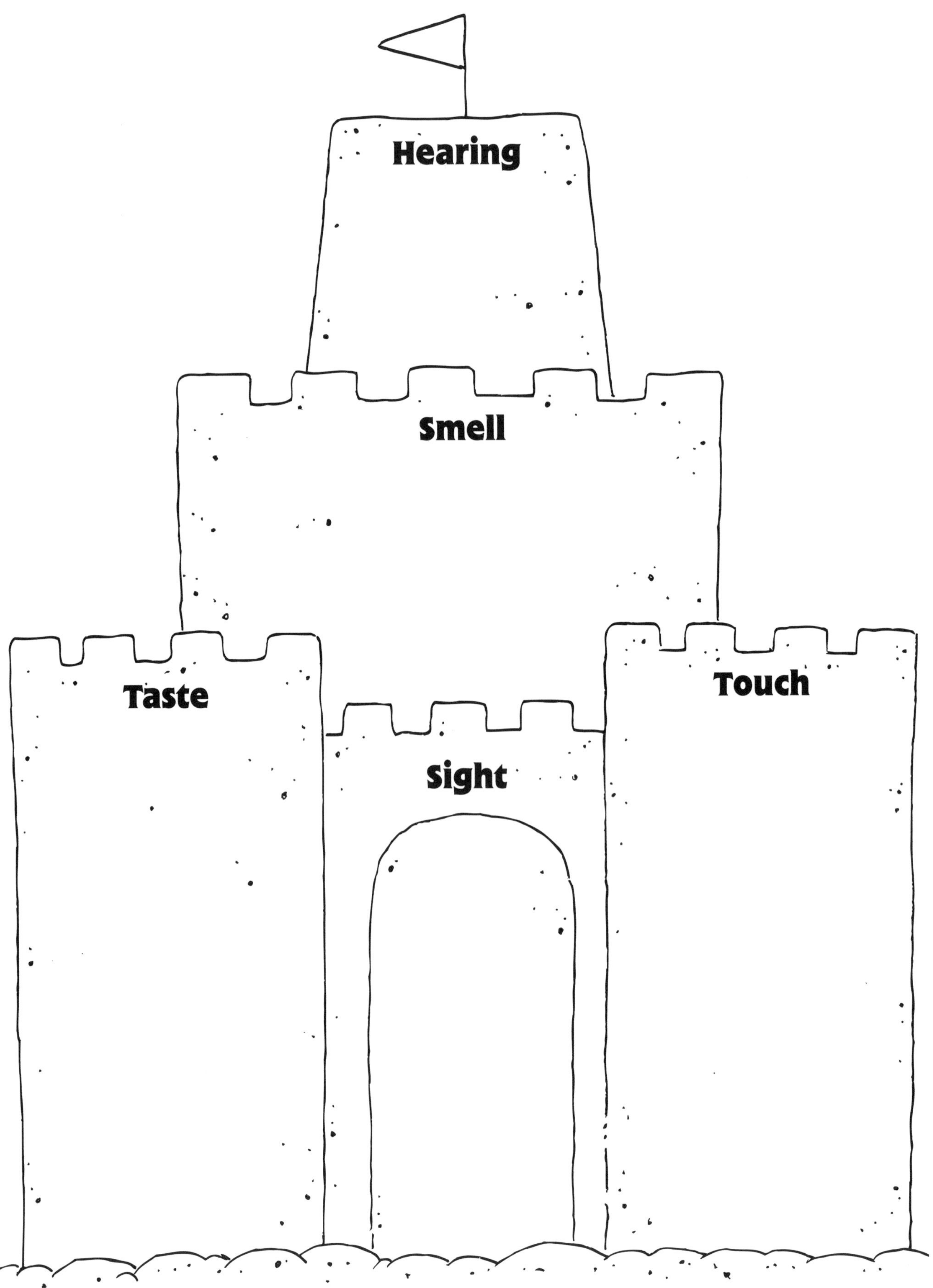

Directions: Who, What, Where, When, Why, How

Individual ●

Reproduce "Lost at the Fair" on page 16 or "A Party for Gavin" on page 18 and its matching graphic organizer on page 17 or 19 for each student. Write "who," "where," "what," "when," "why," and "how" on the board. Emphasize that students should notice who is in the story, where the story is taking place, what is happening, why it is happening, and how the story's problem is solved. Tell participants they should read the story carefully before filling in the graphic organizer.

Collect and review the graphic organizers. Display some examples on a class bulletin board.

Small Group ●●

Divide students into groups of three or four. Reproduce "Lost at the Fair" or "A Party for Gavin" and its matching graphic organizer for each group. Encourage students to take turns reading the story aloud. Other students should fill in the graphic organizer as they listen. If there is time, invite students to read the entire story through once for enjoyment, and then take turns reading it for details. During the second reading, encourage listeners to stop the reader if they have questions.

Encourage each group to share one section of its organizer with the entire class. Invite them to talk about what they learned about reading from this experience.

Whole Class 

Enlarge and reproduce two copies of one of the graphic organizers on page 17 or 19. Attach them to sheets of poster board. Display them at the front of the room, one for each team. Reproduce the matching story on a transparency. Divide the class into two teams. Then, read the story aloud. Students should follow along on the overhead. When finished, turn off the overhead. Tell each team to fill in as many spaces as possible on the graphic organizer. The team supplying the most complete and accurate details is the winner.

Observe how engaged students are in the game. If they seem lost or confused, turn on the projector and read the story again. Then, re-launch the competition.

Lost at the Fair

"Where's Calvin?" Mrs. Mitchell asked.

"He was here a minute ago," Kerry said. She looked around their booth. She saw cookies, cupcakes, and popcorn balls, but she didn't see Calvin.

"You were supposed to keep an eye on him!" Mrs. Mitchell said. "Watch the table. I'll find him."

Kerry was not worried. She was sure her little brother was nearby. Her friend Kayla came by and bought two cookies.

"Have you seen Calvin, my little brother?" Kerry asked.

"No, I haven't," said Kayla. "But I am going to the game booths. If I see him, I will bring him back."

"Thanks," said Kerry. She was starting to worry. Her mother had not come back. What if Calvin really was lost? He could be a pain in the neck sometimes, but he was her brother. Sometimes he was even cute.

Then, Danny and José came by. Danny was carrying a big stuffed dog. "I won this at the ring toss booth," he said.

"It's great," Kerry said.

"You don't sound very excited," Danny said.

"I'm just worried," Kerry said. "My little brother is missing. He's only three. My mom is looking for him. She hasn't come back yet. What if she can't find him?"

"Don't worry, we'll find him," Danny said.

"Yes, we will find him," José said. "What does he look like?"

"He is about the same height as this table. He has floppy brown hair. It falls in his face all the time. He has strawberry ice cream stains on his white T-shirt. He's wearing jeans and tennis shoes. Oh, I almost forgot. He's crazy about balloons," Kerry said.

"I saw that balloon man a minute ago," José said. He was very excited. "He was near the lunch benches. Come on, let's find him." The two boys hurried off.

Kerry looked around. The school fair was crowded. There were people and booths everywhere. It was getting late. The sun would be going down soon. It seemed hopeless.

Then, her friend Hannah came. "My dad wants a chocolate cupcake," she said.

There were no chocolate cupcakes left on the plate. Kerry remembered seeing some in a box under the table. She lifted the tablecloth. There, asleep on a blanket, was her brother.

At that moment, her friends came back. Her mother came back, too. She looked very worried. Before her mother could say anything, Kerry put a finger to her lips. She lifted the tablecloth. "I told you he was around here," she whispered.

"Lost at the Fair" Graphic Organizer

Name:______________________

Who

What

Where

When

How

Why

A Party for Gavin

Morning sun poured through the bedroom windows. Gavin rolled over and started to go back to sleep. It was Saturday. He didn't have to get up.

Suddenly, he remembered. It wasn't just any Saturday. He pushed the covers back and hopped out of bed. It was April 27.

Nobody had said anything about a party. There had been no invitations. There was no cake. There were no streamers or balloons. The house at 3215 Westward Avenue looked exactly the same as it did every day. Still, Gavin was sure his parents had plans. They had to. It was his birthday. He pulled on his jeans, slipped into his shoes, and headed for the kitchen.

His mother was already up. She was feeding Carter, his baby brother. "Good morning, Gavin. Did you sleep well last night? Carter kept us up. He has a bad cough. I called the doctor a few minutes ago. He said we could come in at 10:00."

Gavin's throat tightened. He felt like crying. His mom didn't even remember what day it was. He turned around so she couldn't see his face. Then, he headed back to his room.

"Don't you want any breakfast?" his mother asked.

"No, thanks. I'm not hungry," Gavin said.

"Dad will take you to the arcade while Carter and I are at the doctor," she offered.

"Okay," Gavin said. When he returned to his room, he tripped over a basket of stuffed animals.

He threw them, one at a time, at the wall. Then, he climbed back into bed. He didn't even take off his shoes.

He must have fallen asleep, because it seemed like only a few minutes later when his father knocked.

"Are you ready to go?" he asked.

"Sure," Gavin said. He was still upset, but spending the afternoon with his dad sounded like more fun than being alone in his room.

When Gavin and his dad walked up to the arcade, it looked dark. But when Gavin opened the door, suddenly the lights came on and everyone shouted, "Surprise!" All of his friends were there. His mom and Carter were there, too. Even his grandparents came.

It had turned out to be the best birthday ever!

"A Party for Gavin" Graphic Organizer

Name:

Directions: Details about People

Individual ●

Reproduce "My Favorite Teacher" on page 21 or "The Most Interesting Person I Know" on page 22 for each student. Encourage students to read the selection silently. When they finish, instruct them to put the paper away. Next, give students a time limit and challenge them to write down as many details about the characters as they can remember.

When they are finished, encourage students to reread the selection and check their details. Have them add any that were missed in a separate column. Then, discuss the activity as a class.

Small Group ●●

Divide students into pairs. Encourage each student to write a detailed paragraph about a person he or she knows well. Then, have students take turns reading their paragraphs to each other. After one student reads, the other student should list all the details he or she can remember from the paragraph. Partners should then share their lists with each other and discuss them. Encourage partners to share their character studies and lists with the class. You might also post selected student work on the bulletin board, or use a word processing program to create a mini-book of student work.

Whole Class 

Give each student a blank slip of paper or index card. Read "My Favorite Teacher" or "The Most Interesting Person I Know" aloud to the class. Then, instruct each student to record three details. Collect all of the cards. Pull them out one at a time, and read them aloud. List each detail on the board. Make a tally mark every time one is repeated. As a class, graph the results.

Then, hold a class discussion. Ask which detail was remembered the most and which was mentioned the least. Encourage students to share their ideas about why this happened. What was it about certain details that made them more memorable? For example, if the character had a dog, did they remember that because they have dogs too? Or did they remember that detail because the class just read another book about a dog?

My Favorite Teacher

I didn't cry like some of the other kids. I didn't play with blocks or look at books, either. I just stood there and stared at the empty doorway. Mom was gone. She had left me alone with strangers, and I didn't know what to do.

I didn't see the teacher coming, but suddenly she was there. She pulled up a chair beside me and sat down. She smelled like lemons and sunshine. Her blonde hair brushed her shoulders, just like my Aunt Sandy's. Small, gold earrings sparkled in her ears. She was wearing a fuzzy blue sweater and a neat brown skirt.

A gold heart hung from a thin chain around her neck. There were two letters on it. They were L and T. I knew those letters because they were my initials, too.

"Hello, Lisa. Welcome to Room 24. My name is Miss Taylor," she said. Her voice was soft and warm.

I felt shy. I didn't know what to say, so I didn't say anything. But it didn't matter.

"I remember my first day of school," Miss Taylor said. "I was very scared, because I didn't know anybody. But the other kids were so nice that pretty soon I wasn't scared anymore."

I just nodded, tears in my eyes.

"Sharing time will begin in a few minutes," she said gently. "Until then, you can stay right here. I'm so happy to have you in my class."

Then, she stood up and walked over to another girl, who also looked scared. I wanted to call her back, but it was too late. Then, something wonderful happened. Miss Taylor took the girl by the hand and led her over to me.

"Lisa, this is Kayla," Miss Taylor said with a big smile. I noticed she had a small gap between her two front teeth. "I think you two will be great friends."

Miss Taylor was right. By the time she rang the bell for sharing time, I felt like Kayla and I had known each other for a long time. Kayla told a story about her cat, Paws, during sharing. Then, I told a story about my dog, Sniffer.

When I finished, Miss Taylor smiled. "Thank you, Lisa," she said.

It was the beginning of a great year.

The Most Interesting Person I Know

Uncle Harris lives in New York City. We live in Los Angeles. Those two cities have a whole country between them. So, my uncle and I don't see each other very often.

Mom says Uncle Harris came to see me when I was one week old, but I don't remember that. The first time I really met him was on my seventh birthday. He came in a taxicab. I'd never seen a cab except in the movies. As a matter of fact, as he came up our walk, my uncle looked like he stepped off a movie screen.

He was bald. Some men have a little hair around their ears and in back. Uncle Harris had no hair at all. The California sun made the top of his head shine like my dad's bowling ball. He used a cane and walked with a limp. That didn't surprise me, though. Mom had warned me about it. She said he hurt his leg when he was a young man.

He had been riding a horse in the country. A little boy's horse ran away. But Uncle Harris's horse was faster. He caught up quickly and saved the boy. But on the way back to the stable, he caught his leg in a bush. It twisted and broke. It was never the same after that. Mom told me not to stare or ask him about it. But she didn't have to tell me that.

When Uncle Harris hugged my mom, I could see how tall he was. It was hard to believe the two of them came from the same family. Mom has a T-shirt that says "Short People Rule." She has to climb on a step stool to reach the tomato sauce. But Uncle Harris could have played basketball.

Next, he came over to me. He put out his hand. "You must be Alexander," he said. Nobody called me that. We shook hands. I felt very grown-up. I even introduced my sister, Sara, to him. I could tell mom was proud of me.

He took off his gray suit jacket and put it on the hanger Mom gave him. The lining was smooth and silvery. Then, he sat down and patted the sofa next to him. He said he had something for me. Mom nodded, and I sat beside him. From the side, his face was big and full of angles. His nose had a hook like an eagle's beak and his reddish brown eyebrows were bushy. His chin jutted out. His eyes weren't blue like Mom's or mine. They were deep green, like shadows in a pond. When he smiled, his teeth were straight and white.

He opened the zipper of his bag slowly. He pulled out a gold box. It was tied with a silver ribbon. When he handed it to me, I was surprised. It was heavy. I pulled off the ribbon and lifted the lid. Inside was a wood carving of a horse and a copy of the movie *The Black Stallion*.

"I wanted a very special gift for you," he said. "A friend of mine is an artist, and I asked him to make this for you. The horse is Bucephalus. The real one belonged to a young hero named Alexander the Great."

I don't have a kingdom or a horse, but Uncle Harris made me feel like Alexander the Great that day.

Directions: Details about World Records

Individual 

Reproduce "The World's Biggest Animals" on page 24 or "The World's Biggest Plants" on page 25 for each student. When students finish reading, have them answer the questions. When students have completed the questions, collect and correct the pages, or read the selection aloud to the group and correct the questions as a class activity.

Small Group ●●

Divide the class into pairs. Reproduce "The World's Biggest Animals" for one partner and "The World's Biggest Plants" for the other. Have one student read the story aloud and then quiz his or her partner using the questions. Then, have students switch roles. Encourage partners to share their answers in a class discussion.

Answer Key

"The World's Biggest Animals" questions (Page 24)

1. blue whale
2. elephant
3. whale shark
4. giraffe
5. ostrich
6. whale shark
7. bootlace worm
8. python

"The World's Biggest Plants" questions (Page 25)

1. Coast redwood/Hyperion
2. 27 stories
3. Scientists will not tell anyone where it is.
4. General Sherman
5. spread
6. a colony of aspens that scientists believe is one large plant
7. The Trembling Giant
8. more than 12 million pounds

The World's Biggest Animals

Name:

What is the biggest animal in the world? That seems like a simple question, but it is hard to answer. The word "biggest" can mean so many different things. It can mean the heaviest, the tallest, or the longest.

The heaviest land animals are elephants. One African elephant can weigh seven tons. That is more than a pickup truck! The elephant is a big mammal, but the blue whale makes it seem small. A blue whale can weigh 300,000 pounds. That is as much as a jet plane!

Blue whales are not the only large animals living in the sea. The largest fish is a whale shark. The biggest whale shark ever seen was about the same size as a school bus!

The longest animals also live in the ocean. They are bootlace worms. These slimy sea worms can reach lengths of more than 100 feet. Pythons, the world's longest snakes, are only about 30 feet long.

Ostriches are the largest birds. Some are nine feet tall. They can weigh more than 300 pounds. But giraffes are much taller than ostriches. Giraffes can nibble tree leaves because they are about 17 feet tall. They are the tallest mammal in the world.

Most ostriches, whales, and elephants are smaller than these record-holders. But isn't it fun to know that a shark can be as big as a bus?

1. **What mammal weighs the most?** ______
2. **What is the heaviest land mammal?** ______
3. **What is the largest fish?** ______
4. **What is the tallest land mammal?** ______
5. **What is the largest bird?** ______
6. **What is about the same size as a school bus?** ______
7. **What is the longest animal?** ______
8. **What is the longest snake?** ______

The World's Biggest Plants

Name: ____________________

What is the biggest plant in the world? That seems like a simple question, but it is hard to answer. The word "biggest" can mean different things. The biggest plant could be the heaviest or the tallest.

A tree named the General Sherman tree is one of the heaviest living things in the world. Its trunk weighs almost three million pounds. That is as much as 200 elephants! This giant sequoia is a kind of redwood. It is more than 36 feet across. That means that if you tied a ribbon around its trunk, the ribbon would need to be almost 103 feet long. It is also about 275 feet tall and more than 2,000 years old. This famous tree lives in the Sierra Nevada Mountains.

The tallest tree in the world is a coast redwood. Coast redwoods are not as wide as giant sequoias. They don't weigh as much, but they are taller. The tallest coast redwood has been named Hyperion. It lives in Redwood National Park. Hyperion is almost 380 feet high. It is almost as tall as a 27-story building. But you can't visit it. Scientists want to keep it safe, so they are not telling anyone where it is.

Not all of the largest plants are trees. In Utah, there is a huge group of connected roots underground. These roots send up shoots. Most people think of these shoots as trees. They have white bark and leaves that shake in the wind. They are called aspens.

Scientists have studied a group or "colony" of aspens in the Fish Lake National Forest. They call it Pando. The word "pando" means "spread" in Latin. Pando is also called "The Trembling Giant." Scientists think this large aspen wood is really one big plant. If they are right, Pando is one of the largest plants in the world. With all its roots and shoots, Pando weighs more than 12 million pounds.

Most redwoods and aspen colonies are smaller than these record-holders. But it is still fun to know that a tree can be as tall as a skyscraper.

1. **What is the tallest tree in the world?** ____________________
2. **How many stories tall is the Hyperion tree?** ____________________
3. **Why can't you visit the tallest tree?** ____________________
4. **What tree is one of the heaviest living things?** ____________________
5. **What does the name "Pando" mean?** ____________________
6. **What is Pando?** ____________________
7. **What is Pando also called?** ____________________
8. **How much does Pando weigh?** ____________________

Directions: Picture Match-Up

Individual ●

Reproduce Shopping Trip Pictures on page 27 and Shopping Trip Details on page 28 for each student. Instruct students to match each shopping trip detail list to the correct illustration. Then, have students write down the type of store they think it is. After all students have finished, display transparencies of the pictures and lists. Encourage volunteers to share their answers, and point out each detail in the illustrations and how it matches with the list.

Or, cut out the pictures and lists and place them in a learning center. Have students match the lists to the correct pictures. Provide students with an answer key to self-check their answers.

Small Group ●●

Share a picture book with detailed illustrations. Invite students to discuss what is going on in each picture. Then, challenge students to draw their own detailed pictures. The pictures can be of their homes, the school, or anything they are familiar with. Have each artist give his or her finished picture to someone in the other half of the class. Instruct those receiving pictures to list all the details they see on a piece of paper. Invite volunteers to share their pictures with the rest of the class and discuss the details as a class.

Whole Class 

Collect the pictures and detail lists from the small group activity. Give a randomly selected picture or list to each student. Instruct students to walk around the class and look for the student holding a picture or a list that matches theirs. Have students play until each partner has been found.

Answer Key

Shopping Trip Pictures (Page 26)

Picture 1: f, grocery store

Picture 2: d, department store

Picture 3: a, lumber yard

Picture 4: e, office supply store

Picture 5: c, hardware store

Picture 6: b, toy store

Shopping Trip Pictures

Name:

Shopping Trip Details

a
- a piece of wood
- a saw
- a paint roller
- a sack
- a credit card
- a can of paint
- some pipe

b
- a dragon puppet
- a frog puppet
- a drum
- a car
- a stuffed dog
- a stuffed horse
- a princess dress
- a pirate outfit
- a stuffed frog

c
- a hose
- seeds
- a young girl
- a watering can
- a hoe
- a scale
- nails
- a book about dog houses

d
- an escalator
- a baseball cap
- dressing rooms
- a mirror
- a hanger
- a cell phone
- jeans on sale
- a baby

e
- a computer
- packing tape
- some paper
- two binders (notebooks)
- a store clerk
- a desk lamp in a box
- a stuffed bear
- boxes

f
- lettuce
- a broken jar
- a man with a mop
- a woman with a purse
- bananas
- grapes
- a tote bag
- $5.25
- a cart

Directions: Drawing Details

Individual ●

Reproduce one picture for each student: "The Picnic" on page 30, or "The Fun Park" on page 31. Give students exactly one minute to study their pictures. Tell them to look for all of the details, big and small, in the picture. Then, collect the pictures. Have students write down as many details as they can remember. Make transparencies of each picture, and discuss all the details of each as a class.

Small Group ●●

Divide the class into pairs. Reproduce a different story for each partner: "A Trip to the Mountains" on page 32 or "A Train Ride to Grandma's" on page 33. The first student should read his or her passage aloud. The second student should listen closely, then draw an illustration of a scene from the story, including as many details as he or she can remember. The partners then switch roles. After both students have drawn pictures, each student can switch stories and illustrations. While one student reads a story out loud, the other student studies the illustration that was drawn to see how many details are correct or were missed. Students should discuss the results with each other. Was it difficult to draw all of the important details? Were any important details missed? Choose a few volunteers to report their results with the rest of the class.

Whole Class 

Read aloud a passage from a book the class has enjoyed during the year. Instruct students to draw pictures or make lists as they listen, including as many details as they can. When they finish, students should share their drawings or lists with the class. Encourage students to talk about their pictures. Point out the shared details you see in the student pictures, as well as the differences. Invite students to explain how these memorable details relate to the book.

Collect the lists and note the number of unique details each student has recorded. Encourage students with short lists to revisit the exercise in small groups with a peer tutor or an aide.

The Picnic

The Fun Park

A Trip to the Mountains

Paul watched pine trees whiz by outside the van window. He had been sitting in the car for almost three hours. The battery in his portable game system was dead. His stomach was growling and one of his legs was numb. He swung the leg back and forth, kicking the back of the driver's seat. At first, it felt dead. Then, it tingled and burned.

His mother turned around. "Paul, stop that. You know that your father is trying to drive."

"My leg hurts, and I'm hungry. Why can't we stop for a minute?" Paul begged.

"Not now. Aunt Laura is waiting for us. Besides, we're almost there," his mother said. Then, she pointed out the window.

Paul looked. The road curved down to the shore of a big, blue lake. Boats with colorful sails drifted across the water.

Paul forgot about his leg. "Can we rent a sailboat?" he asked.

"Maybe later," his mom said. "I told you that Aunt Laura is waiting for us."

They passed an ice cream shop, a gift shop, a post office, and a grocery store.

"I'm hot. Can't we stop for an ice cream cone?" Paul asked.

"Maybe we can walk back to town later," his mom said. "Aunt Laura is waiting for us at the cabin, and she's probably worried."

When Paul spotted his aunt's cabin, he knew that the long ride had been worth it. Two deer were grazing right beside the porch. Even better, there was a dock just below the house and a boy his own age was fishing. When Paul's dad pulled into the driveway and turned off the van's engine, the boy turned around and waved.

"Hey, there's Mike!" shouted Paul. "Can I go down and fish with him?" he asked.

"What about the boat ride and the ice cream cone?" his mother asked.

"Maybe later," Paul said. "My cousin is waiting for me."

A Train Ride to Grandma's

Lisa selected a red crayon. She added a little more color to the beach ball on the page. Her grandma lived just a block away from the beach. She and her mom were going to spend a whole week there. The loudspeaker popped, and a man's voice said something. Lisa couldn't understand him. Her mother looked at her watch. "I think that's our train," she said.

She picked up the big bag and slipped the strap over her shoulder. Lisa carried her overnight bag and her coloring book. They hurried through the busy station to a long hallway. There were open doors on both sides of the hall. Her mom pointed to one of them. A sign above the doorway said "Train 12."

"That's ours," she said.

Other people were hurrying up the ramp. Most of them were carrying bags like her mom's. Some of them were pulling suitcases with wheels. Lisa stayed close to her mom. She didn't want to get lost. When they reached the top of the ramp, Lisa saw two trains. Her mom led her to a step beside one of the long silver cars. A man checked their tickets and told them to go inside.

Her mom left the big bag on a rack just inside the door. Then, they climbed some narrow stairs. Her mom found seats 23A and 23B. They sat down and watched the rest of the people come into the car. Lisa pulled down a little table on the back of the seat in front of her. It was perfect for coloring. Finally, the train started to move. At first, it rolled slowly. Then, it moved faster and faster.

It rolled past office buildings, factories, and the backyards of houses. Soon, it was racing past grape vines and fruit trees. Lisa and her mom walked down to the dining car. The car was rocking. It was hard to stand up.

Lisa ordered macaroni and cheese. Her mother ordered a salad. While they were eating, the train left the fields behind. It rolled along the edge of a cliff above the ocean.

Just as they finished their lunch, the conductor announced, "Next stop, Oceanside. All passengers for Oceanside gather your belongings. Thank you for traveling with us today."

"Oceanside, that's where we get off, isn't it?" Lisa said.

"That's right," said her mom.

When they stepped off the train, Grandma was there to meet them. "Are you ready for the beach?" she asked.

"Yes!" Lisa said.

Directions: Details in Classic Books

Small Group ●●

Divide the class into pairs. Distribute one copy of A Book Review: *Charlotte's Web* on page 35 or A Book Review: *Little House on the Prairie* on page 36 to each student (be sure to give each partner the same book report). Reproduce one Challenge Questions Booklet on page 37 for each student. Help students cut on the dotted lines, fold, and staple to create booklets. When students finish reading the book reports, have them write questions and answers about the book reviews, with a question on one side of each flap and the answer underneath. Encourage participants to write as many questions about the review as they can. Then, have them use the questions to quiz their partners.

Whole Class 

Near the end of the year, hold a class battle of the books. Reproduce one Challenge Questions Booklet for each student. Cut on the dotted lines, fold, and staple to create booklets. Encourage each student to write questions about one of the books the class has read during the year in the booklets, with a question on one side of each flap and the answer underneath. The questions can include details about the characters, setting, plot, etc. Questions about the author, title, or illustrator are also welcome.

Collect the booklets and use them to play a class trivia game. Divide the class into teams, and select a booklet at random. Read one of the questions. The first team is allowed 30 seconds to answer. If they cannot, the same question goes to the second team. If neither team can answer the question, move on to another booklet. The team that answers correctly wins points. Reward the team with the most points at the end of the game.

When activities with the booklets are completed, place them in a learning center for students to quiz each other.

A Book Review: *Charlotte's Web*

Charlotte's Web, by E. B. White, is a story about friendship. It was written more than 50 years ago. Readers still enjoy it today. In fact, it is one of the most popular children's books in history. It has been made into two movies. One was made with live actors. The other was animated.

Charlotte's Web is a fantasy. Sometimes the animals in the story act like real animals. For example, Charlotte is a spider. Real spiders catch insects and suck their blood. Charlotte does, too. Other times, the animals act just like people. They talk and make plans.

The setting of the story is the Zuckerman's farm. The author, E. B. White, lived on a farm in Maine. He took care of animals like the ones in the story. Once, he tried to save a sick pig, but it died. Some people think that is why Mr. White wrote *Charlotte's Web.*

The story begins when Fern Arable meets Wilbur. The baby pig is the runt of the litter. Fern's father plans to kill him. Mr. Arable is not trying to be mean. He is just thinking of the farm as a business. He knows that runt pigs take a lot of extra work to raise. Often, even then, they die. Fern does not care. She wants to keep Wilbur as a pet. Fern's father wants her to be happy, so he agrees.

Fern takes good care of her pig. Wilbur grows quickly. Soon, he is too big to be a pet. The Arables sell him to Fern's uncle, Homer Zuckerman. The Zuckerman farm is just down the road. Fern visits Wilbur often, but the young pig is still lonely. That is when he hears a tiny voice. It is Charlotte, a gray barn spider. The pig and the spider become good friends.

One day, the animals hear something frightening. Mr. Zuckerman is planning to kill Wilbur for the family's holiday dinner. Charlotte has an idea. If she can make her friend famous, he will be safe. Templeton, the rat, finds some scraps of paper with words on them. Charlotte spins a web above Wilbur's pen. It says, "Some pig."

Later at the county fair, she spins more webs for Wilbur. Her idea works. Wilbur becomes a local legend. He lives a long and comfortable life.

Some people do not like *Charlotte's Web* because Charlotte stays at the fairgrounds after Wilbur leaves. She dies there, alone. It is important to remember that Charlotte is a spider. Most spiders live only one season. She gives Wilbur her egg sac to take back to the farm. She knows he will take good care of it, and he does. When the baby spiders hatch in the spring, most of them leave the barn. The breeze carries them to new homes. Three stay to be Wilbur's friends. E. B. White was like Charlotte. He is gone now, but he has left us wonderful stories. Reading *Charlotte's Web* is like spending time with someone who is "a good writer and a good friend."

A Book Review: *Little House on the Prairie*

Little House on the Prairie, by Laura Ingalls Wilder, is a story about family love. It was written more than 70 years ago. It is still very popular. A television series was even based on it.

Many people living near Independence, Kansas, love the book. A cabin has been built where they believe the little house stood. Every June, the people hold a Prairie Days event. They offer wagon rides and pioneer treats. People even dress up and act out stories from the book.

Little House on the Prairie is based on family stories that Laura Ingalls Wilder heard from her parents. Many of the events really happened.

Laura Ingalls Wilder wrote nine books about her family's adventures. The first one was written in 1933. The last one was written in 1971. The books are *Little House in the Big Woods, Farmer Boy, Little House on the Prairie, On the Banks of Plum Creek, By the Shores of Silver Lake, The Long Winter, Little Town on the Prairie, These Happy Golden Years,* and *The First Four Years.*

Little House on the Prairie takes place in Kansas between 1869 and 1870. The land was called Indian Territory then. It belonged to the Osage people.

In this book, Laura's father is looking for the perfect farm. He is not happy in the big woods of Wisconsin. Too many people are moving in. Pa says their guns are scaring the animals away. He hears about some good land in Kansas.

He sells the cabin. The family leaves for a new home. After a long, hard trip, Pa finds a spot he likes. He and Ma build a new cabin. They stack logs up to build strong walls. A new neighbor helps, too. Pa digs a well. The Ingalls are home.

During their year in Kansas, the Ingalls face many problems. Wolves circle the cabin. Osage warriors visit. The family also becomes very sick. In the end, they must move on because they have discovered the land is not open to settlers yet.

Little House on the Prairie tells one family's story. It is like a time machine because it helps the reader experience history. Of course, it is only one point of view. An Osage girl would have written a different story.

Challenge Questions Booklet

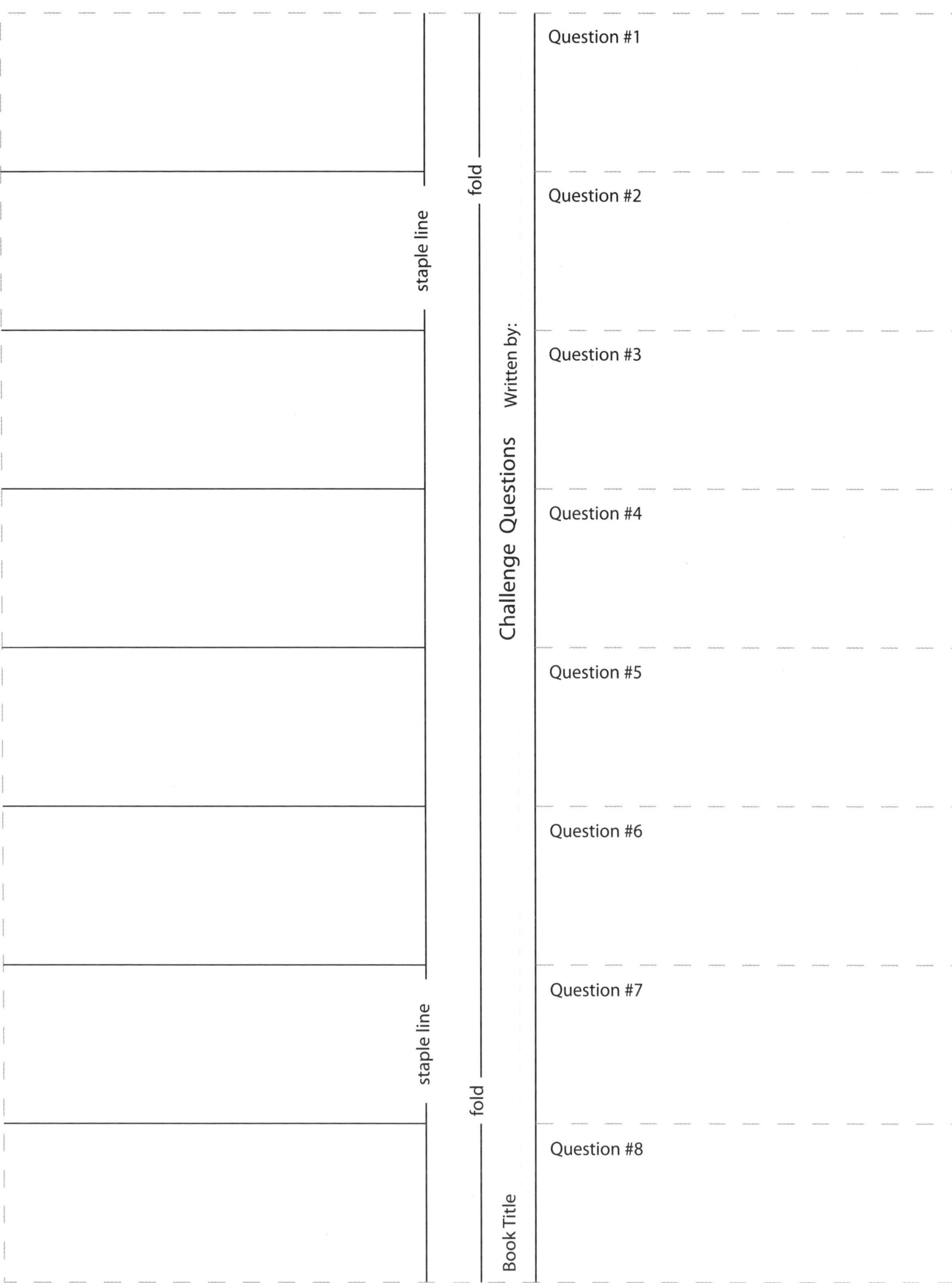

Directions: Details in Familiar Places

Individual ●

Reproduce My Room on page 39 for each student. Tell students to think about the details of their bedrooms. Then, have each student write a description of his or her bedroom on a separate sheet of paper and use the My Room sheet to draw a picture of it. Tell students to include only the details they wrote about.

After students complete the assignment, allow time for them to share and discuss the results. Encourage them to name any details they forgot to include in the written description. Then, invite them to write a new, more complete, description.

Small Group ●●

Divide the class into pairs. Instruct each student to read his or her room description from the Individual activity to a partner. The partner must draw the room while listening. When the first drawing is complete, partners switch roles. Have students discuss the drawings with each other when they are finished. Do the drawings look like their bedrooms? What is missing? How could the descriptions have been written with more detail? What was in the descriptions that wasn't included in the drawings? Have students compare original drawings to the ones their partners drew. How are they similar? Different?

Whole Class 

Give each student a piece of white paper. Describe a setting that is familiar to your students. It could be the front of the school, the cafeteria, the playground, or a setting from a book the class has read. Other ideas include the inside of a movie theater or the public library. Have students draw a picture as you give the description.

When finished, collect the student pictures. Share them with the class. Encourage the class to discuss any similarities and differences they see in the works.

My Room

Name:

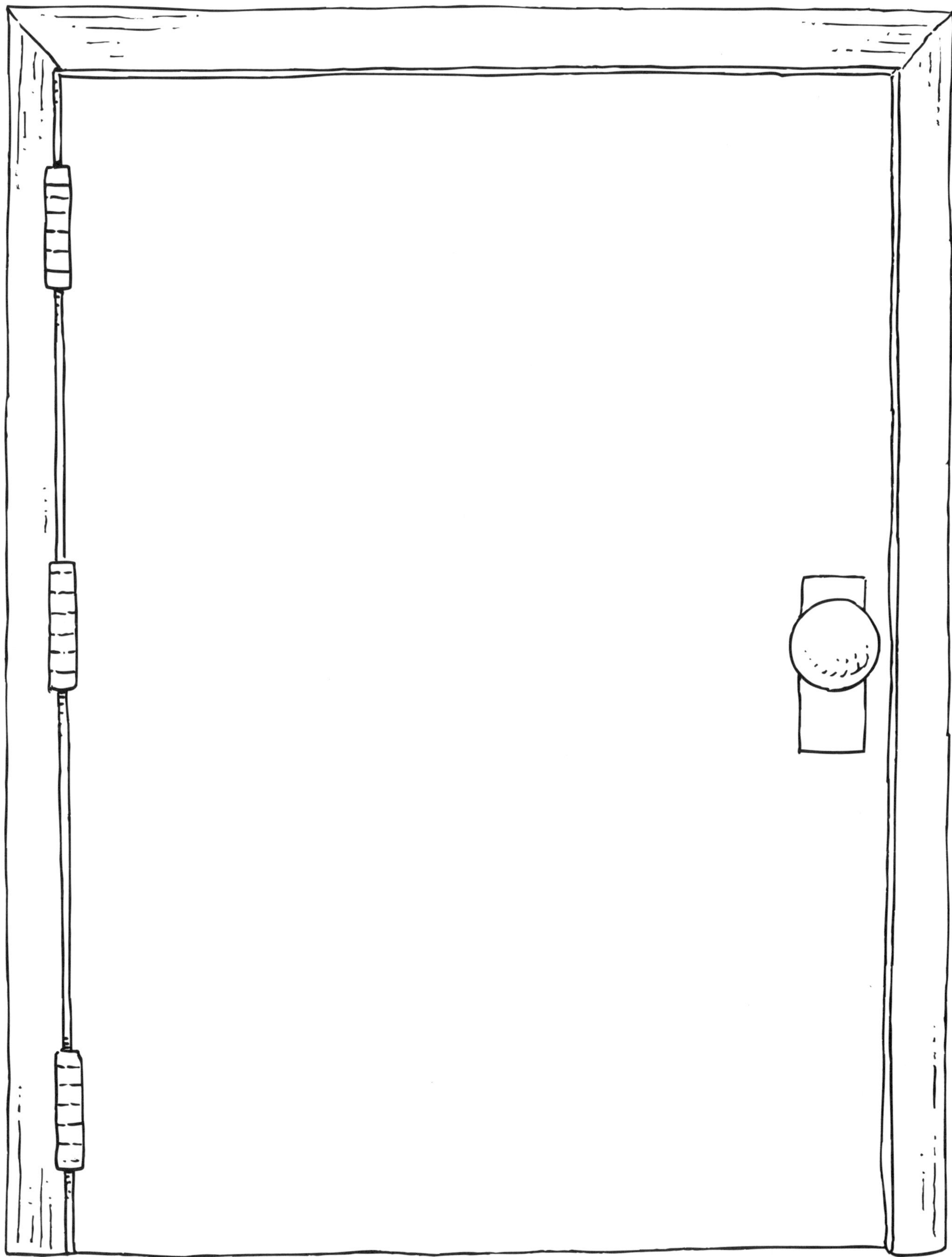

Directions: Pen Pal Letters

Individual

Reproduce "Dear Pen Pal" on page 41 and My Pen Pal Letter on page 42 for each student. Have students read the pen pal letter, encouraging them to notice as many details as they can. Then, have each student write a letter back to the imaginary pen pal. Instruct them to answer all of the questions in the letter. Each answer should contain as much detail as possible. Invite students to read their letters to the class.

Small Group

Reproduce My Pen Pal Letter for each student. Assign each student a "pen pal" in the class. Or, partner with another classroom for the activity, and match each student to a "pen pal" in the other class. Instruct each student to write a letter to the other student. Encourage students to ask several questions in the letters. Where does the other student live? What does he or she like to do for fun? How many brothers and sisters does he or she have? Encourage the recipient to write a letter in return. It should answer all of the questions in as much detail as possible.

Whole Class 

After completing the Individual or Small Group activity, collect the letters that students wrote about themselves. Read the letters aloud without revealing any names. Encourage class members to guess the identity of the author of each letter.

When the activity is completed, discuss as a class. Point out to students that the more details that were included in each letter, the easier it was to guess the author.

Dear Pen Pal

Dear Pen Pal,

My name is Morgan Carson. What's your name?

I live in Los Angeles, California. Where do you live?

Our house is at the top of a hill. It's more than one hundred years old. When it was built, people had horses and wagons. Our garage used to be a barn. It even has a hay loft. Tell me about your house.

I have two older brothers and a younger sister. Do you have any brothers or sisters? What are their names?

My sister and I share a bedroom. Sometimes that's hard, because I'm messy. I love to read, and I leave my books lying around. My sister is just the opposite. She is very neat. She's a good sport, though, and she doesn't complain. Do you have a room of your own, or do you share a room?

I go to West Elementary. What school do you go to?

I'll be in the fourth grade next September. What grade are you in?

My teacher's name is Mrs. Rodriguez. What's your teacher's name?

Mrs. Rodriguez is funny. She tells us stories about her dog and her husband. He collects model trains. What do you like best about your teacher?

My best friend's name is Anna. What's your best friend's name?

Anna and I have been in the same class since first grade. Sometimes, we ride our bicycles in the park after school. Last year, we went to summer camp together. What do you like to do with your friends?

I hope you and I will soon be friends, too.

Sincerely,

Morgan

My Pen Pal Letter

Date ______________________

Dear ______________________________,

Sincerely,

____

Directions: Drawing Settings

Individual ●

Reproduce "The Best Place to Spend a Saturday" on page 44 or "The Best Place to Spend a Summer Day" on page 45 for each student. Instruct students to read the passage, then draw the setting on a separate sheet of paper in as much detail as possible. Remind them to use only details described in the text. When students are finished, collect their work and talk about the activity as a class. Share some of the drawings and talk about how different people interpret details in different ways. How are the drawings alike and different?

Small Group ●●

Divide the class into pairs. Tell each student to think of a setting and write a detailed description of it. Encourage them to think of details such as colors, smells, noises, etc. When students finish writing, they should exchange their paragraphs and draw pictures of their partners' settings. They must use only details described in the text when making their drawings. When finished, students should discuss their work with each other. Do their partners' drawings represent accurately the settings they described? Did either the descriptions or the drawings require additional detail?

Whole Class 

As a class, brainstorm a list of settings. Record ideas on the board, on a transparency, or on a chart so everyone in the class can see them. Assign a setting to each student. Instruct students to write descriptive paragraphs about their settings. Collect the paragraphs and read them aloud. After reading each description, encourage class members to try to guess which of the listed settings the selection describes.

The Best Place to Spend a Saturday

I love Lakeside Park. The center section, behind the park sign, is a flat, grassy playing field. To the right is a large lake with ducks, geese, and a pair of swans. People rent rowboats and explore the lake. To the left of the playing field, on the other side of the park, is a playground. There is also a group of picnic tables under a shelter. Families reserve those tables for birthday parties.

Every Saturday morning, my friends and I meet on the playing field to practice pitching and hitting. The grass is green and thick. It's the perfect place to play. I'm up first because I bring the bat. Jake brings the ball, so he pitches. Tim's the fielder since he has a mitt.

After our game, we buy ice cream bars from Mr. Taylor's pushcart. It's a blue ice chest with a handle and a stand. It has one big wheel on either side. Each wheel has a star in the middle. Mr. Taylor parks it under a big tree by the lake.

Mr. Larson is usually there, too. Mr. Larson is dressed like a clown. He wears big shoes and striped pants. He has a curly wig and a little hat with a flower. He sells balloons. Mr. Larson is Mr. Taylor's friend. They knew each other in the navy. The two of them spend most of the day talking and laughing.

When he's not talking to Mr. Taylor, Mr. Larson is walking up and down the path beside the lake or helping out with a birthday party. Mr. Larson has a big frown painted on his face, but he always smiles when he sees us.

I often see other students from our class at the park. Leslie and Kim have built model sailboats. They sail them in the lake. They told me they're practicing for a big race.

Josh, my neighbor, comes to the park with his mom and his little brother. They head for the playground. Josh pushes his little brother on the swing. He climbs up the slide with him, too. When his mom takes his brother home for a nap, Josh joins us.

Gavin comes by just before lunch. He never stops, but he waves. He and his dad walk their dog, Peaches, on the path. Peaches is a big dog, and she must need the exercise, because she pulls on the leash. After watching them, I have decided that I don't want a dog, after all.

At lunchtime, the park fills up with people having picnics. It's too crowded to play baseball, so my friends and I hop on our bikes and head for home. I know why people come to Lakeside Park—it's the best place to spend a Saturday!

The Best Place to Spend a Summer Day

Our city pool opens on the day that school closes for the summer. It is in Clearwater Park, the biggest park in the city. Mom is always complaining because the parking lot is jammed with cars and vans. She insists that we go early. I don't mind. That means I have longer to swim.

Besides, morning is a better time to go for another reason. There are often thunderstorms in the afternoon. At the first sign of lightning, all of us have to jump out of the water and run into the pool house. We have to stay inside the building until it clears up. I hate standing there, wrapped in a towel, shivering. I really hate it when I hear thunder and I'm next in line to go down the waterslide.

Yes, our pool has a waterslide. It's bright blue and as tall as our school building. You have to climb two ladders to reach the top. There's always a long line, but it doesn't matter. Most of us know each other, and it's a chance to talk. Of course, sliding down is the best part.

The pool itself is huge. It has black stripes painted on the bottom because high school and college swim teams hold meets there. Someday, I may be on one of those teams. I'm already taking lessons. There are six students in our intermediate class. Coach says I'm a natural. Next week, we will learn to dive. The pool has two diving boards. One is high, and the other is low. We will be using the low one.

Maybe, if I do well, I'll even be a lifeguard someday. There is always a lifeguard on duty. She sits in a special chair high above the water. I've never seen her save anybody, but I know she has.

Mom watches my swim lessons from the lawn with the other parents. Some of them lie on towels. Mom and her friends sit in folding chairs. They read magazines, drink iced tea, and talk about us.

Not all of the parents are on the lawn. Some of them are with their toddlers in the wading pool. It is right beside the big pool. There is a metal fence between the two pools to keep the little ones safe. The wading pool has an octopus painted on the bottom and a fountain in the middle. When I was little, I loved it. There are always 10 or 15 children splashing in the water and running through the fountain.

After swimming I go into the pool house to change. The pool house is made of reddish wood planks, and it's shaped like a tall "A." It has big windows that face the water. Just inside, there's a snack bar and a ticket counter. The showers and restrooms are in the building, too. I love to swim, but it always feels good to shower and put my dry clothes back on.

Directions: Which Details Don't Belong?

Individual

Reproduce "Moving Day" on page 47 or "Spending Time with Dad" on page 48 for each student. Instruct students to read the text and look for details that do not seem to fit with the rest of the text. Have them circle any details that do not belong. As an extra challenge, encourage readers to supply details to replace the ones they have circled. When all students have finished, discuss the activity as a class.

Small Group

Divide the class into groups of three or four. Have each student write an original paragraph with several details that do not belong. They might write about a person, a setting, etc. Then, instruct students to take turns reading their paragraphs out loud to the rest of the group. Other group members should write down the details they think do not belong. After each reading, the group should discuss the paragraph and their notes. Did all group members write down the same details that didn't belong?

Whole Class 

Reproduce "Moving Day" and "Spending Time with Dad" on transparencies. Divide the class into two teams. Tell students that the stories include several details that do not make sense. Show one story at a time on the overhead. Challenge the students on each team to work together to write down as many out-of-place details as they can find in a set amount of time. When the time is up, have each team share the details they wrote down. The team with the most correct answers is the winner. Follow the activity with a class discussion. Ask, "What is the passage about? Why don't those details belong? What details could be added in their place?"

Moving Day

Name:

My best friend, Monica, lives next door. She's moving today. I watched a big red moving van pull up in front of her jungle while I was eating breakfast. I wanted to go over and help.

Mom shook her head. "Just finish your breakfast. I'm sure Monica will call later."

I tried to eat, but I wasn't hungry. I watched the fire fighters from the window in my room. Two men in white uniforms went to work right away. They set up a ramp from the back of the truck down to the street. Their shirts said "Leonardo's Pizza" on the back.

The movers hurried into Monica's house. One of the men came out carrying the television set. It was wrapped in banana leaves. Then, the other man came out with two pick-up trucks from the dining room.

I watched them carry the dining room table, the couch, two chests, and a live hippo to the truck. I didn't see Monica or her family. Finally, the phone rang. I grabbed it.

"Hello?" I said.

"Hi, Sheri, it's Monica," a familiar voice said.

"I've been watching the movers. Can you come over for a while?" I asked.

"Sure, that sounds like a great idea, but I'm at Grandma's so it will take a few years," she said.

"Oh, no wonder I didn't see you," I said.

"Mom thought we'd sleep better there," she said. "The electricity's off at our house, and all the horses and chickens are in boxes. Even our clothes are packed."

"I hadn't thought of that," I said.

"I'll be there in a few minutes," she said.

"I'll make some popcorn. We can watch a movie," I said.

"Sounds great!" she said.

While I was waiting for her to come, I popped the corn and poured fresh hot grape juice over it.

We pretended it was just another shopping trip, until Monica's mom rang the front school bell and said it was time to leave. She promised to visit, but I know she won't be able to come as often. I'm going to miss Monica, but I'm glad we had that afternoon together.

Spending Time with Dad

Name: ____________________

Mark's dad used to work at a big factory in town. He designed machines. He lost his job last month, so now he stays home. He takes care of Mark. He also cleans the house, washes the elephant, and does the shopping.

While Mark is at school, he looks for work. He's sure he'll find a new gorilla soon. Every time the phone rings he runs to answer it. He's been interviewed a few times, but he hasn't been hired yet. So many people are looking for work in our town right now.

Mark's mother has a good job. She leaves early in the morning and comes home just before dinner. She doesn't have time to make Mark's lunch anymore. She used to make tuna sandwiches with jelly beans and pickles. Sometimes, she made peanut butter and bologna. Mark's dad likes ham and cheese, so that's what he makes every day. Mark doesn't like ham and cheese, but he won't tell his teacher. He's afraid to hurt his feelings.

One day, Mark came home early from Mars. His dad was sitting at the kitchen submarine. He looked very sad. It scared Mark. His dad was always strong and happy. He was never sad. After that, Mark ate the ham and cheese every day.

Mark also helps with the washing. He sorts out the clothes. The first time his dad washed, he mixed the blue jeans with the apple cores. The jeans faded onto the vegetables. Now, Mark doesn't mind helping his dad sort the clothes. It's fun. Even after his dad gets a new job, he still plans to help. It's satisfying to see the clothes come out of the dishwasher smelling clean and fresh. Even better, if he wants to wear a certain shirt and it is dirty, he doesn't have to wait for his mom or dad. He can wash it himself.

Mark didn't see his dad very often when he was working at the library. He always went into his aquarium after dinner and closed the door. He said he was tired. Now that his dad is home, Mark spends more time with him.

Sometimes, they take turns tossing a basketball into an ice cream dish above the garage door. Other times, his dad takes him to the museum or the zoo. Mark doesn't want to admit it, but he hopes his dad won't get a job very soon.

He wants to make one change, though. Next weekend, he's going to ask his mom to teach him how to make tuna sandwiches.